PALEO COOKBOOK

SNACKS EDITION

Paleo Snacks Recipes
with Easy Instructions

Jamie Evans

TABLE OF CONTENTS

"BREADED" PALEO CHICKEN CUTLETS {WHOLE30}

Crispy "breaded" Paleo Chicken Cutlets that are super easy and just as good as the original. Whole30 compliant, kid friendly!

MAKES 6 SERVING/ TOTAL TIME 15 MINUTE

INGREDIENTS

1.5 lbs boneless skinless chicken breasts, thin sliced or pounded to 1/2" thickness
1 cup blanched almond flour*
1/4 cup coconut flour*
1 and 1/4 tsp fine grain sea salt
1/8 tsp black pepper
2 tsp Italian seasoning blend <--My favorite
1 tsp onion powder
1/2 tsp garlic powder
dash red pepper flakes optional
1 egg whisked
3 tbsp coconut oil + 2 tbsp ghee for frying**

METHOD

STEP 1

Mix all the dry ingredients in a medium shallow bowl (you will dredge the cutlets in the mixture)
Have your whisked egg in a shallow bowl, heat a large, heavy, deep skillet over medium heat and add 3 tbsp total of cooking fat (a combination of ghee and coconut oil, or all coconut.) Depending on the size of your skillet, you might have to fry these in 2 batches, so have additional cooking fat ready in case you need more.

STEP 2

Once the skillet it preheated (you can see if a drop of the dry mixture sizzles), dip one cutlet in the egg, shaking off excess, then coat in the dry mixture, shaking off excess. Place the chicken in the pan, then repeat the process for each piece of chicken.
Cook on one side until medium-golden brown (2 minutes) and crisp, then carefully turn over the chicken with tongs and cook the second side until golden brown and juices run clear, about 2 minutes depending on the thickness of your chicken***
Carefully remove chicken cutlets from skillet with tongs and place on a paper-towel lined plate to absorb excess grease. Serve hot with baked fries, sweet potatoes, or butternut squash fries! Enjoy!

NUTRITION VALUE

334 cal, 20g fat, 5g saturated fat, 3g fiber, 29g protein, 7g carbs.

CREAMY POTATO CHOWDER WITH SHRIMP AND BACON

This one-pot Creamy Potato Chowder with Shrimp and Bacon is the ultimate comfort food on a chilly evening!

MAKES 6 SERVING/ TOTAL TIME 40 MINUTE

INGREDIENTS

1 package nitrate-free bacon
1 pound deveined shrimp
1 onion, minced
2 garlic cloves
3 Yukon potatoes, diced
2 celery ribs, diced
2 carrots, minced
1/4 teaspoon sweet paprika
1/2 teaspoon dried thyme
4 cups chicken stock
1 cup fresh or frozen corn, thawed and cooked
1/4 cup heavy cream or ¼ cup cashew cream
1 tablespoon fresh parsley, for garnish
1 sprig fresh thyme, for garnish
1 tablespoon scallions, for garnish

METHOD

STEP 1

Heat a large Dutch oven over medium heat. Add bacon and cook until crispy, around 5-8 minutes. Turn off heat and place bacon on a plate lined with paper towels. Drain all but 1 tablespoon of bacon fat out of the pan. Turn heat to medium-high and cook shrimp for about 2-3 minutes on each side, or until pink and fully cooked through.

STEP 2

Place garlic and onion into the Dutch oven. Cook for 1-2 minutes or until onions start to turn translucent. Add potato, celery, and carrots to the pot. Cook until potato starts to soften. Add in spices. Cook for 1-2 minutes, making sure to scrape up all of the brown bits from the bottom of the pan. Cover and bring to a boil over medium-high heat. Once at a boil, add corn and turn down heat and let simmer for 10-15 minutes. Serve in desired serving bowls.

NUTRITION VALUE

266 cal, 11.4g fat, 3.8g saturated fat, 3g fiber, 23.7g protein, 14g carbs.

CREAM OF ZUCCHINI SOUP

An easy summer soup that will use up a bountiful of zucchini if you have them. It can be served chilled or hot, so be sure to try both ways!

MAKES 4 SERVING/ TOTAL TIME 20 MINUTE

INGREDIENTS

1 tablespoon olive oil

1 onion diced

4 zucchini diced

2 cloves garlic minced

1 teaspoon dried thyme

1 cup chicken broth

1 cup heavy cream

Fresh chopped basil leaves for serving

Sea salt and fresh ground pepper to taste

METHOD

STEP 1

Heat the oil in a pot and add the onions, zucchini, garlic, and thyme. Cook until softened and add the broth. Bring to a boil, and simmer for 5 minutes.

STEP 2

Transfer to a blender and blend until smooth; add back to the pot and add the cream. Simmer for 5 minutes. Serve topped with the basil.

NUTRITION VALUE

289 Kcal, 20g fat, 3g fiber, 20g protein, 11g carbs.

SHRIMP AND VEGGIE CHOWDER

An easy and healthy soup that is creamy and delicious. Full of protein and fiber, it will become a regular on your dinner table.

MAKES 4 SERVING/ TOTAL TIME 20 MINUTE

INGREDIENTS

1 tablespoon olive oil

1 pound shrimp chopped

1 onion diced

2 stalks celery diced

1 bell pepper diced

2 cloves garlic minced

1 carrot diced

1 zucchini diced

1 tablespoon Old Bay seasoning

2 cups chicken broth

1 cup heavy cream or coconut milk

Sea salt and fresh ground pepper to taste

METHOD

STEP 1

Heat the oil in a large pot. Add the shrimp and cook until pink. Remove from pot.

STEP 2

Add the veggies and Old Bay and cook until softened and lightly browned. Add the broth and cream and bring to a low simmer.

Simmer for 10-15 minutes, and add the shrimp back to the pot. Heat through and serve.

NUTRITION VALUE

421 Kcal, 20g fat,
2g fiber, 32g protein, 9g carbs.

CHICKEN FAJITA SOUP

Made with chicken thighs for richer flavor, this easy to make soup will satisfy your cravings for fajitas but without all the carbs!

MAKES 4 SERVING/ TOTAL TIME 30 MINUTE

INGREDIENTS

1 tablespoon olive oil

3 bell peppers sliced

1 onion sliced

2 cloves garlic minced

1 teaspoon cumin

1 teaspoon chili powder

1 teaspoon oregano

1 teaspoon paprika

4 chicken thighs

6 cups chicken broth

Juice of 1 lime

Chopped cilantro diced avocado, sour cream, for serving

Sea salt and fresh ground pepper to taste

METHOD

STEP 1

Heat the oil in a large pot. Add the peppers, onions, garlic, and seasonings. Cook until softened and add the chicken and broth.

STEP 2

Bring to a boil and reduce to a simmer. Simmer until chicken is cooked through. Remove and let cool slightly. Shred and add back to the pot.

Add the lime juice and simmer for 5 minutes.

Serve topped with desired accompaniments.

NUTRITION VALUE

331 Kcal, 18g fat,
2g fiber, 26g protein, 8g carbs.

CAULIFLOWER SHAKSHUKA

Shakshuka is an easy dish to make when you want to impress, but it's also nutritious and delicious. This version, with the addition of cauliflower is hearty and filling. This is the perfect healthy brunch recipe for lazy weekends.

MAKES 2 SERVING/ TOTAL TIME 20 MINUTE

INGREDIENTS

2 tablespoons olive oil

1 onion chopped

1 cup cauliflower florets

3 cloves garlic minced

2 tablespoons tomato paste

1 teaspoon ground cumin

1/2 teaspoon smoked paprika

1 28- ounce can crushed tomatoes

6 large eggs

2 ounces crumbled feta

2 tablespoons chopped fresh parsley

Sea salt and fresh ground pepper to taste

METHOD

STEP 1

Preheat oven to 350 degrees F.

In a large straight sided skillet or braising pan, heat the oil. Add the onion and cauliflower and cook until soft and lightly browned. Add the garlic, tomato paste, and seasonings and cook for another minute. Add the tomatoes.

STEP 2

Make six small wells in the tomatoes and crack the eggs into each one. Season with salt and pepper and top with the feta.

Bake for 10-15 minutes, until egg whites are set and yolks are slightly firm. Remove from oven and sprinkle with parsley before serving.

NUTRITION VALUE	616 Kcal, 20g fat, 14g fiber, 32g protein, 14.9g carbs.

PUMPKIN SPICED PALEO GRANOLA

Eat with almond milk and fruit, or sprinkle a bit on top of high quality yogurt. It also makes a delicious and addictive snack.

MAKES 12 SERVING/ TOTAL TIME 45 MINUTE

INGREDIENTS

1/8 cup coconut oil melted

1/4 cup honey

1/2 cup pecans

1/2 cup walnuts

1/2 cup sliced almonds

1/2 cup unsweetened coconut flakes

1/2 cup sunflower seeds

1/2 cup pumpkin seeds

3 tablespoons sesame seeds

3 tablespoons flax seeds

1 tablespoon pumpkin pie spice or season to taste

1/2 teaspoon sea salt

1/2 cup dried cranberries

METHOD

STEP 1

Preheat oven to 350 degrees F.

Combine the coconut oil and honey in a large bowl and whisk until combined. Add the nuts, seeds, pumpkin pie spice, and salt, and stir to coat well.

STEP 2

Spread mixture on a parchment or foil lined baking sheet. Bake for 30-40 minutes, until brown and fragrant. Remove from oven and stir in the cranberries. Let cool, then break up, or put in a food processor and pulse for a more traditional granola like texture.

This recipe makes about 4 cups. Store in an airtight container.

NUTRITION VALUE	245 Kcal, 18g fat, 3g fiber, 20g protein, 15g carbs.

CHILI ROASTED CASHEWS

In addition to a simple snack, you can throw these chili roasted cashews in a salad, sprinkle on soup, or add to a stir-fry.

MAKES 8 SERVING/ TOTAL TIME 45 MINUTE

INGREDIENTS

2 cups raw cashews

1 tablespoon light olive oil

2 teaspoon chili powder

1 teaspoon honey

Juice of 1 lime

1/2 teaspoon sea salt

METHOD

STEP 1

Preheat oven to 350 degrees Line a baking sheet with parchment paper.

Put all of the ingredients in a freezer bag and shake until cashews are well coated. Spread evenly on the baking sheet.

STEP 2

Bake for 20-25 minutes until cashews are golden and fragrant. Allow to cool completely before serving. Store in an airtight container.

NUTRITION VALUE	181Kcal, 14g fat, 1g fiber, 19.9g protein, 10g carbs.

GUACAMOLE DEVILED EGGS

Deviled eggs get a redo with creamy avocado and fresh salsa. Make up a batch and then grab a couple when you need a quick snack.

MAKES 1 2 SERVING/ TOTAL TIME 20 MINUTE

INGREDIENTS

6 hardboiled eggs

1 avocado pitted and peeled

1 clove garlic minced

1/2 small tomato diced

1 tablespoon minced jalapeno

2 tablespoons red onion diced

2 tablespoons chopped cilantro

Juice of 1 lime

Sea salt and fresh ground pepper to taste

METHOD

STEP 1

Peel the hardboiled eggs and remove the yolks. Add them to a bowl with the avocado and mash.
Add the remaining ingredients and mix well.

STEP 2

Spoon the mixture into the egg white halves. If saving for later, put the guacamole mixture in an airtight container and spoon into the eggs when ready to eat.

NUTRITION VALUE	62 Kcal, 4g fat, 1g fiber, 4g protein, 2g carbs.

COCONUT CREAMED CUCUMBERS

The coconut milk and cucumbers in this easy side dish get a punch of heat from the pepper. This easy summer side dish is great for a backyard barbecue.

MAKES 4 SERVING/ TOTAL TIME 30 MINUTE

INGREDIENTS

2 cucumbers sliced

1/2 cup coconut milk

1 teaspoon lemon juice

1 teaspoon fresh ground black pepper

1 teaspoon fresh chopped dill

Sea salt to taste

METHOD

STEP 1
Combine all of the ingredients in a large bowl. Let stand at room temperature for 20 minutes or so to develop the flavors. Serve at room temperature or chilled.

NUTRITION VALUE	653 Kcal, 9g fat, 8g fiber, 46g protein, 14g carbs.

HOT PEPPER ROASTED BROCCOLI

Broccoli is one of those veggies that takes on new life when roasted in a hot oven. The edges become crisp, and the flavor comes alive in a way that it doesn't when steamed.

MAKES 4 SERVING/ TOTAL TIME 40 MINUTE

INGREDIENTS

1 head broccoli cut into florets

3 tablespoons olive oil

1 teaspoon crushed red pepper flakes

Juice of 1 lemon

Sea salt and fresh ground pepper to taste

METHOD

STEP 1

Preheat oven to 425 degrees F.

Toss all of the ingredients until broccoli is well coated, and spread evenly on a baking sheet.

Roast for 30-40 minutes, stirring once or twice, until broccoli is charred and tender. Serve immediately.

NUTRITION VALUE

467 Kcal, 20g fat,
1g fiber, 48.1g protein, 3.4g carbs.

TUNA CUCUMBER BITES

These easy no-cook appetizers come together fast, and they taste delicious. The tuna salad can be made ahead of time and everything can be put together right before you need it.

MAKES 1 SERVING/ TOTAL TIME 20 MINUTE

INGREDIENTS

2 (5 oz) cans high-quality tuna drained

1/2 cup finely minced onion

2 cloves garlic minced

2 tablespoons fresh chopped dill

1 tablespoon lemon juice

2 seedless cucumbers thinly sliced

Sea salt and fresh ground pepper to taste

METHOD

STEP 1

Combine the tuna, onion, garlic, dill, and lemon juice in a bowl and mix well.

Lay the cucumber slices on a sheet tray or serving platter and top with the tuna mixture. Serve at room temperature.

NUTRITION VALUE	625 Kcal, 20 fat, 11g fiber, 54.2g protein, 14 carbs.

SPICED APPLE PEAR SAUCE

Pears give the usual applesauce a new dimension of flavor. Better than anything you'll buy in the store, this is perfect for breakfast, as a side, or used in baked goods.

MAKES 1 SERVING/ TOTAL TIME 6 HOUR

INGREDIENTS

3 large apples peeled and cored

3 large pears peeled and cored

2 cinnamon sticks

1/8 teaspoon fresh grated nutmeg

1 teaspoon vanilla

Pinch of salt

METHOD

STEP 1

Put everything in your slow cooker and cook over low heat for 6-8 hours.

STEP 2

Mash well or blend in a food processor or blender. Cool completely, and store in a jar in the fridge

NUTRITION VALUE	358 Kcal, 20g fat, 4.5g fiber, 26.1g protein, 11.6g carbs.

MARINATED RAW FETA

This easy appetizer is rich and flavorful and couldn't be easier to make. Serve with olives, sundried tomatoes, and high quality cured meat for amazing appetizers your guests will love.

MAKES 1 SERVING/ TOTAL TIME 30 MINUTE

INGREDIENTS

8 ounces raw feta cheese sliced into 1/2" slabs

1 cup extra-virgin olive oil

2 cloves garlic smashed

2 sprigs fresh mint

2 sprigs fresh oregano

1 lemon juiced

1 teaspoon whole peppercorns

1 teaspoon crushed red pepper flakes optional

METHOD

STEP 1

Lay the cheese in a shallow container. Add the remaining ingredients, making sure the cheese is covered by the oil.

Cover and refrigerate for several hours, but up to 3 days. Serve at room temperature.

NUTRITION VALUE	498 Kcal, 20g fat, 3.9g fiber, 21.7g protein, 15g carbs.

BONE BROTH

Homemade bone broth is loaded with nutrients, but is not a quick process. With your Instant Pot, that changes. This easy recipe is versatile, nutritious, and perfect for soups, stews, or even just drinking out of a mug on a cold day.

MAKES 8 SERVING/ TOTAL TIME 2 HOUR

INGREDIENTS

3 pounds bones of your choice chicken, beef, or pork, or mix

1 onion halved

4 stalks celery

2 carrots peeled and cut into chunks

Fresh herbs: parsley rosemary, or thyme

lemon juiced

Water

1 tablespoon kosher salt

METHOD

STEP 1

Put the bones in your instant pot with your veggies, herbs, and lemon juice.

Cover with about 8 cups of water, but don't fill your pot more than about 2/3 full. Add salt.

STEP 2

Lock the lid and cook at high pressure for about 2 hours. Use the natural release to release the pressure.

Allow to cool and strain the broth. Store in sealed containers in the fridge, or freeze for longer storage.

NUTRITION VALUE

464 Kcal, 20g fat, 20.8g fiber, 43g protein, 8g carbs.

CURRIED ROASTED CAULIFLOWER

Spicy and flavorful, this easy side dish adds exotic flair to anything you serve it with.

MAKES 4 SERVING/ TOTAL TIME 30 MINUTE

INGREDIENTS

1 head cauliflower cut into florets

1/2 cup fresh or frozen peas

1 tablespoon curry powder

2 tablespoons coconut oil

Sea salt and fresh ground pepper to taste

METHOD

STEP 1

Preheat oven to 400 degrees F.

Toss the cauliflower and peas with the curry and coconut oil. Lay on a baking sheet and roast for 30 minutes, or until tender.

Serve immediately.

NUTRITION VALUE

197 Kcal, 13g fat, 5.8g fiber, 10g protein, 14.8g carbs.

PALEO SLIDERS

You don't need a bun to have a delicious slider. If you're serving these at a party, stick toothpicks in them so guests can easily pick up and go.

MAKES 1 SERVING/ TOTAL TIME 30 MINUTE

INGREDIENTS

1 pound grass-fed ground beef

1/2 pound ground veal

1 egg

1/4 cup almond flour

2 cloves garlic minced

1/4 cup finely minced onion

1 teaspoon Italian seasoning

METHOD

STEP 1

Mix all of the ingredients in a bowl using your hands, being careful not to over mix.

STEP 2

Form into 2-inch patties, and cook in a skillet until cooked through. Serve with your favorite Paleo condiments like mayo or mustard.

NUTRITION VALUE	197 Kcal, 13g fat, 5.8g fiber, 10g protein, 14.8g carbs.

SALMON STUFFED AVOCADOS

Mini avocados make perfect appetizers or snacks when stuffed with savory ingredients like salmon and veggies.

MAKES 4 SERVING/ TOTAL TIME 10 MINUTE

INGREDIENTS

6 oz can wild caught salmon drained

1/4 cup onion diced

2 tablespoon minced pimentos

1 tablespoon olive oil

1 tablespoon chopped fresh parsley

Juice of 1 lemon

2 mini avocados

METHOD

STEP 1

Combine the salmon, onion, pimentos, olive oil, parsley, and lemon juice in a small bowl. Mix well.

When ready to serve, cut the avocados in half and remove the pit. Fill the avocado halves with the salmon mixture right before serving.

NUTRITION VALUE

200 Kcal, 10g fat,
10g fiber, 20g protein, 15g carbs.

OVEN APPLE CHIPS

If you're looking for something crispy, healthy, and flavorful, these apple chips will hit the spot. They're easy to make, don't require any special equipment, and are super addicting. Use your favorite kind of apple, or a mix.

MAKES 4 SERVING/ TOTAL TIME 2 HOUR

INGREDIENTS

4 apples any kind

1 teaspoon ground cinnamon

METHOD

STEP 1

Preheat oven to 200 degrees F.

Core the apples and thinly slice using a sharp knife or mandolin. The thinner your slices, the crispier the apple chips will be.

STEP 2

Lay on baking sheets in a single layer, sprinkle on cinnamon, and bake for 1 hour. Flip, and continue baking until crisp.

Let cool completely, and store in an airtight container.

NUTRITION VALUE	354 Kcal, 17g fat, 10g fiber, 33g protein, 14g carbs.

FRESH SUMMER SALSA

When fresh tomatoes abound, salsa is the perfect party food. It's quick, flavorful, and easy to customize. This makes a good Paleo party food when served with crunchy veggies, but it's also a great topper for grilled chicken or fish.

MAKES 1 SERVING/ TOTAL TIME 10 MINUTE

INGREDIENTS

4 large tomatoes diced

1 green bell pepper diced

1 red onion diced

1 small bunch cilantro chopped

2 cloves garlic minced

1 teaspoon ground cumin

Juice of 2 limes

1 tablespoon avocado or olive oil

Sea salt and fresh ground pepper to taste

METHOD

STEP 1

Combine all of the ingredients in a large bowl and toss until well combined. Refrigerate until ready to serve to allow the flavors to meld.

NUTRITION VALUE	335 Kcal, 14g fat, 8g fiber, 32g protein, 15g carbs.

COCONUT YOGURT

This is one of the recipes using your Instant Pot that isn't exactly instant, but it is worth the trouble.

MAKES 8 SERVING/ TOTAL TIME 3 HOUR

INGREDIENTS

3 cans coconut milk refrigerated overnight

1 5- gram package dairy-free yogurt starter

Honey maple syrup, or other Paleo-approved sweetener, optional

METHOD

STEP 1

Without shaking the coconut milk, open the cans, and scoop out the thickened cream that has settled on top. Add this to your Instant Pot.

Press the "yogurt" setting on your pot to bring your cream to a boil. When your mixture is boiling, turn off your pot.

STEP 2

Let the mixture sit at room temperature until it reaches 100 degrees F, and then add a tiny bit of your starter, and whisk until smooth. Keep adding the starter in small amounts and whisking until smooth.

STEP 3

Turn the pot back on to the yogurt setting, and set the timer for 6-8 hours. The longer you let it go, the tangier the flavor will be.

STEP 4

When done, whisk in honey or maple syrup to taste. Transfer to an airtight container and refrigerate for 6-8 hours, until thick and creamy.

NUTRITION VALUE	335 Kcal, 14g fat, 8g fiber, 32g protein, 15g carbs.

POMEGRANATE CABBAGE SALAD

This winter salad is crisp, bright, and delicious, and perfect as a hearty side dish. The bright tangy dressing brings it all together and makes it shine.

MAKES 4 SERVING/ TOTAL TIME 20 MINUTE

INGREDIENTS

4 cups shredded cabbage red, green, or mixture

1 shredded carrot

1/4 cup chopped parsley

1/2 cup pomegranate arils

1/2 cup olive oil

3 tablespoons white wine vinegar

1 teaspoon Dijon mustard

1 teaspoon maple syrup or pomegranate molasses

Sea salt and fresh ground pepper to taste

METHOD

STEP 1

Put the cabbage, carrots, parsley, and pomegranate arils in large bowl and toss well.

Whisk the remaining ingredients in a small bowl or shake in a jar and toss with the salad before serving.

NUTRITION VALUE

625 Kcal, 20 fat,
11g fiber, 54.2g protein, 14 carbs.

CHORIZO STUFFED JALAPEÑOS

These easy appetizers are big on flavor, especially for those that like heat. If you like extra hot, you can swap habaneros for the jalapeños.

MAKES 4 SERVING/ TOTAL TIME 30 MINUTE

INGREDIENTS

1/2 pound chorizo

1 teaspoon ground cumin

1/2 teaspoon oregano

2 cloves garlic

4 jalapeno peppers halved lengthwise, seeds removed

sea salt and fresh ground pepper to taste

METHOD

STEP 1

Preheat oven to 350 degrees F.

In a medium skillet, cook the sausage with the spices and garlic until no longer pink.

STEP 2

Lay the peppers cut side up on a baking sheet. Fill with the sausage mixture.

Bake for 10-15 minutes, until peppers are lightly softened and browned.

Serve warm.

NUTRITION VALUE

459 Kcal, 20g fat,
4g fiber, 20g protein, 14.2g carbs.

SAVORY GRAIN FREE CRACKERS

These savory grain-free crackers will fulfill your need for that crunch.

MAKES 6 SERVING/ TOTAL TIME 1 HOUR 30 MINUTE

INGREDIENTS

1 cup raw almonds

1/4 cup flax seeds

1 cup Walnuts

1 teaspoon crushed red pepper flakes

1 teaspoon Garlic powder

2 sun dried tomatoes

3 Egg whites

1/2 teaspoon Sea salt

METHOD

STEP 1

Preheat oven to 300 degrees F.

Put all of the ingredients in a food processor. Pulse until you have a dough; don't over process.

STEP 2

Line a baking sheet with parchment paper. Spread the mixture on the parchment as thin as you can. Bake for 1 hour. Remove from oven and allow to cool.

When cool, break into crackers. Store in an airtight container.

NUTRITION VALUE

353 Kcal, 15g fat,
8g fiber, 35g protein, 15g carbs.

SALSA VERDE SOUP

This Salsa Verde soup is spicy, tangy, and rich, and is the perfect appetizer to a Paleo taco night. It's also great served with a taco or fajita salad as a light meal.

MAKES 4 SERVING/ TOTAL TIME 30 MINUTE

INGREDIENTS

2 tablespoons olive oil

1 Onion diced

1 clove garlic minced

2 Jalapeños seeded and minced

1 teaspoon Ground cumin

1 can diced green chilies

1 pound tomatillos paper removed, chopped

6 cups Chicken broth

Juice of 1 lime

Garnishes of your choice: diced peppers or onions sour cream, fresh chopped cilantro

METHOD
STEP 1
Heat the oil in a large pot. Add the onions, garlic, and peppers and cook until soft. Add the cumin and cook for 1 minute.

STEP 2
Stir in the chilies, tomatillos, and broth and bring to a boil. Simmer for 10 minutes, and transfer to a blender to puree.
Stir in the lime juice, and serve with your desired toppings.

NUTRITION VALUE

353 Kcal, 10g fat, 58g protein, 14g carbs.

HOLIDAY MEATBALL BITES

These bite sized appetizers will keep your guests happy while they wait for the main dish. And there are no breadcrumbs required for this Paleo version.

MAKES 10 SERVING/ TOTAL TIME 40 MINUTE

INGREDIENTS

2 pounds Ground beef

1 pound Ground pork

1 Onion finely diced

2 cloves garlic minced

1 tablespoon Italian seasoning

2 Eggs

1/2 cup Almond flour

2 cups Crushed tomatoes

Fresh basil for serving

Sea salt and fresh ground pepper to taste

METHOD

STEP 1

Preheat oven to 400 degrees F.

Combine all of the ingredients except the tomatoes in a large bowl. Mix until just combined.

STEP 2

Line a large baking sheet with parchment paper and form the mixture into 2 inch balls. Dollop each with a teaspoon or two of crushed tomatoes and bake for 20-30 minutes, until browned. Remove from oven and sprinkle with basil.

Insert with toothpicks to make an easy appetizer.

NUTRITION VALUE	163 Kcal, 10g fat, 4g fiber, 20g protein, 12g carbs.

ROASTED THANKSGIVING CARROTS

Carrots are rich in Vitamin A. Vitamin A is an antioxidant that is highly beneficial for our eyesight.

MAKES 6 SERVING/ TOTAL TIME 45 MINUTE

INGREDIENTS

2 pounds baby rainbow carrots tops removed

2 tablespoons olive oil

Sea salt and fresh ground pepper to taste

Crumbled feta or goat cheese to serve, optional

METHOD

STEP 1

Preheat oven to 375 degrees F.

Toss the carrots with the olive oil and lay on a baking sheet. Roast for 20-30 minutes until browned and tender. Remove from oven and serve topped with cheese if desired.

NUTRITION VALUE	480 Kcal, 20g fat, 10g fiber, 20g protein, 14g carbs.

ROASTED BABY SWEET POTATOES

Roasted baby sweet potatoes have concentrated sweet potato flavor, so you don't need much else to make them tasty.

MAKES 4 SERVING/ TOTAL TIME 45 MINUTE

INGREDIENTS

2 pounds baby sweet potatoes halved

1/4 cup olive oil

1 teaspoon Honey

Seasonings of your choice: cumin chili powder, cinnamon, red pepper flakes

Sea salt and fresh ground pepper to taste

METHOD

STEP 1

Preheat oven to 400 degrees F.

Toss the potatoes with the olive oil, honey, and any seasonings you may like. Season with salt and pepper and lay on a baking sheet.

STEP 2

Roast for 20 minutes, flip and continue roasting for 10-15 more minutes, until browned and tender. Serve warm.

NUTRITION VALUE

241 Kcal, 20g fat,
13.6g fiber, 21g protein, 11g carbs.

BROILED BRUSSELS SPROUTS WITH BACON

Tossed in olive oil and topped with bacon, these sprouts are loaded down with satiating fats.

MAKES 6 SERVING/ TOTAL TIME 20 MINUTE

INGREDIENTS

2 pounds Brussels sprouts halved

2 tablespoons olive oil

8 bacon slices cooked and crumbled

Sea salt and fresh ground pepper to taste

METHOD

STEP 1

Put the sprouts in steamer basket or microwave and steam until just tender. Remove and let cool slightly.

STEP 2

Toss the steamed sprouts with the olive oil and a pinch of salt. Lay on a parchment lined baking sheet, cut side up. Preheat broiler to high heat and broil until tops are well browned.
Toss with the bacon and serve warm.

NUTRITION VALUE	181Kcal, 14g fat, 1g fiber, 19.9g protein, 10g carbs.

RASPBERRY ORANGE SORBET

Ditch the store-bought sorbet and make this one instead. It tastes good and it's good for you. That's a win-win.

MAKES 2 SERVING/ TOTAL TIME 10 MINUTE

INGREDIENTS

2 sliced frozen bananas

1 cup frozen strawberries

Zest and juice of 1 orange

1/4 cup Raw honey

METHOD

STEP 1

Put all of the ingredients in a blender and blend until smooth, pressing down with a tamper if necessary. Serve immediately.

NUTRITION VALUE

352 Kcal, 20g fat,
1g fiber, 36g protein, 2g carbs.

MANGO ORANGE SPRITZER

Soda can be a hard habit to quit. Despite all the negative evidence stacked against it, kicking the soda habit is not an easy thing to do.

MAKES 4 SERVING/ TOTAL TIME 10 MINUTE

INGREDIENTS

1 quart sparkling water

Juice of 1 orange

1 ripened mango pitted, peeled, and cubed

METHOD

STEP 1
Combine the water, orange juice and mango in a quart sized jar with a lid. Chill until ready to serve.

NUTRITION VALUE

323 Kcal, 10g fat,
8g fiber, 36g protein, 15g carbs.

GRILLED FRUIT SALAD

The high heat and hot grate caramelizes the fruit, making it sweeter, so you don't even need dessert.

MAKES 4 SERVING/ TOTAL TIME 20 MINUTE

INGREDIENTS

2 ripened peaches pitted and cubed

1/2 pint Strawberries hulled and halved

1 Mango peeled, pitted and cubed

1 cup cubed cantaloupe

1/2 cup toasted walnuts

1/4 cup Coconut cream thickened cream on top of a can of coconut

Juice of 1 lime

Fresh chopped mint for garnish

METHOD

STEP 1

Thread the fruit onto skewers to make grilling easier. Preheat a gas or charcoal grill to medium heat.

STEP 2

Remove from heat and transfer to a bowl with the walnuts.

Divide between plates.

Whisk the coconut cream and the lime juice together and top the salad. Garnish with mint leaves.

NUTRITION VALUE

323 Kcal, 10g fat,
8g fiber, 36g protein, 15g carbs.

BLUEBERRY SODA

Blueberries provide the base for this soda. That means that it will not only leave you feeling refreshed, but it also has some incredible health-promoting qualities.

MAKES 2 SERVING/ TOTAL TIME 10 MINUTE

INGREDIENTS

1 pint Blueberries

2 cups still water

3 cups sparkling water

Juice of 1 lemon

METHOD
STEP 1

Put the blueberries in a blender with the still water and blend until smooth. Add to a pitcher with the sparkling water and lemon juice. Chill until ready to serve.

NUTRITION VALUE

335 Kcal, 14g fat,
8g fiber, 32g protein, 15g carbs.

SMOKED SALMON CUCUMBER BITES WITH LEMON COCONUT CREAM

Easy to prepare and put together, you'll be amazed at how fast these disappear.

MAKES 8 SERVING/ TOTAL TIME 15 MINUTE

INGREDIENTS

2 Cucumbers sliced

1/2 cup Coconut cream (thickened cream on top of a can of coconut)

1 Lemon juiced

4 ounces smoked salmon

2 tablespoons Capers

1 tablespoon minced chives

METHOD

STEP 1

Lay the cucumbers out on a platter or baking sheet in a single layer. Whisk the coconut cream with the lemon juice and top each cucumber slice with a small dollop. Top with smoked salmon, capers, and chives before serving.

NUTRITION VALUE

253 Kcal, 10g fat,
7g fiber, 46g protein, 15g carbs.

CHILLED STRAWBERRY LAVENDER SOUP

Strawberries aren't usually turned into soup, but you'll be surprised at how delicious this summer soup is. Use summer berries for best results, and don't go overboard on the lavender.

MAKES 4 SERVING/ TOTAL TIME 20 MINUTE

INGREDIENTS

1 14 oz can Coconut milk

1 pint Fresh strawberries hulled

Juice of 1 orange

1/2 tsp culinary lavender leaves

1 cup Water

Sea salt to taste

Fresh ground black pepper to taste

METHOD

STEP 1

Put all of the ingredients in a blender. Blend until smooth and creamy. Transfer to an airtight container and chill overnight for best results.

Serve chilled, topped with sliced strawberries if desired.

NUTRITION VALUE

335 Kcal, 14g fat, 8g fiber, 32g protein, 15g carbs.

BACON WRAPPED DATES

This recipe makes the perfect snack. With just the right combination of sweet and salty, it's easy to put together. Make these for a party and watch them disappear fast.

MAKES 12 SERVING/ TOTAL TIME 15 MINUTE

INGREDIENTS

24 pitted dates

24 raw almonds

24 slices bacon cooked until crisp and cooled

METHOD

STEP 1
Stuff each of the dates with an almond. Wrap with a bacon slice and secure with a toothpick if necessary. Serve immediately.

NUTRITION VALUE

241 Kcal, 20g fat,
13.6g fiber, 21g protein, 11g carbs.

CURRIED COCONUT CHICKEN SOUP

This spicy and flavorful soup is an easy way to use up leftover chicken, and makes a hearty meal. You can easily substitute shrimp for a change of pace.

MAKES 4 SERVING/ TOTAL TIME 30 MINUTE

INGREDIENTS

2 tbsp olive oil

1 onion sliced

1 carrot peeled and sliced

2 cloves garlic minced

1 tbsp curry powder

4 cups chicken broth

1 can (14 oz) diced tomatoes

2 cups cooked and chopped (or shredded) chicken breast

1/2 cup coconut milk

Juice of 1 lime

1 bunch fresh cilantro chopped

Coconut flakes for garnish

sea salt to taste

fresh ground black pepper to taste

METHOD

STEP 1

Heat the oil in a large saucepan over medium high heat. Add the onion, carrot, and garlic and cook until softened.

Add the curry powder and cook for a minute. Add the broth and the tomatoes, and bring to a boil. Reduce to a simmer and add the chicken, coconut milk, lime juice, and cilantro. Simmer on low for 5 minutes.

Serve the soup hot, sprinkled with coconut flakes if desired.

NUTRITION VALUE

323 Kcal, 10g fat, 8g fiber, 36g protein, 15g carbs.

CITRUS ROMAINE SMOOTHIE

Romaine is not just for salads. This bright and refreshing citrus smoothie is protein packed, fiber filled, and delicious enough to drink every day.

MAKES 2 SERVING/ TOTAL TIME 10 MINUTE

INGREDIENTS

1 banana

1 orange peeled, with white pith removed

Juice and zest of 1 lemon

1/2 cup diced pineapple

1 head Romaine lettuce roughly chopped

1 cup coconut water

1 cup ice

METHOD

STEP 1
Put all ingredients in a blender and blend until smooth and creamy. Serve immediately.

NUTRITION VALUE

163 Kcal, 10g fat, 4g fiber, 20g protein, 12g carbs.

BACON AND CHIVE SCONES

These tender gluten-free scones get their flavor from bacon and chives. Perfect for brunch or an afternoon snack, they prove that you don't have to give up bread to eat healthy.

MAKES 8 SERVING/ TOTAL TIME 30 MINUTE

INGREDIENTS

1 cup blanched almond flour

2/3 cup tapioca flour

1/2 cup Coconut flour

1 tsp Baking powder

1 tsp Baking soda

1/8 tsp Sea salt

4 tbsp cold grass-fed butter cubed

1/2 cup Full fat coconut milk

2 Eggs

4 slices bacon cooked and crumbled

2 tbsp minced chives

METHOD

STEP 1

Preheat oven to 375 degrees F.

Combine all of the flours in a large bowl with the baking powder, baking soda, and salt.

Add the butter and using your fingers, work the butter into the flour until you have a crumbly mixture.

STEP 2

Add the coconut milk and eggs to the mixture and mix well until you have a dough. Add the bacon and chives and mix until just combined.

Line a baking sheet with parchment paper. Using an ice cream scoop, scoop the dough onto the pan. Bake for 14-15 minutes, until tops are lightly browned and scones are firm. Allow to cool before serving.

NUTRITION VALUE

253 Kcal, 10g fat,
7g fiber, 46g protein, 15g carbs.

APPLE SPICE GREEN SMOOTHIE

Loaded with antioxidants, this sweet and spicy smoothie is a great way to start your day. Healthy fat and fiber keep you full, while coconut milk makes it creamy and delicious.

MAKES 2 SERVING/ TOTAL TIME 10 MINUTE

INGREDIENTS

1 Banana

1 Apple peeled and grated

1 cup baby spinach

1/2 teaspoon Cinnamon

1/2 teaspoon cardamom

1 pinch Nutmeg

1 cup Coconut milk

1 cup Ice

METHOD
STEP 1
Put all ingredients in a blender and blend until smooth and creamy. Serve immediately.

NUTRITION VALUE	498 Kcal, 20g fat, 3.9g fiber, 21.7g protein, 15g carbs.

OVEN SWEET POTATO FRIES

Sweet and savory, these sweet potato fries are the perfect side dish to roasted meats, bun-free burgers, or just as a healthy snack.

MAKES 4 SERVING/ TOTAL TIME 45 MINUTE

INGREDIENTS

2 large sweet potatoes, peeled and cut into fries

2 tablespoons olive oil

Sea salt and fresh ground pepper, to taste

Fresh parsley, for serving

METHOD

STEP 1

Preheat oven to 400 degrees F.

Toss the sweet potatoes with the olive oil and a pinch of salt and pepper.

STEP 2

Lay on a baking sheet in a single layer.

Bake for 35-40 minutes, until fries are lightly browned and tender.

Serve hot.

NUTRITION VALUE

625 Kcal, 20 fat,
11g fiber, 54.2g protein, 14 carbs.

MANGO PUMPKIN SMOOTHIE

This is a great way to use up leftover pumpkin from the holidays, or just to add the winter vegetable to your diet year round.

MAKES 2 SERVING/ TOTAL TIME 10 MINUTE

INGREDIENTS

1 frozen banana, cut into chunks

1/2 large mango, cubed

1/2 cup Pumpkin puree

1/2 teaspoon Cinnamon

1/2 cup Coconut milk

METHOD

STEP 1

Put all of the ingredients in a blender and blend until smooth and creamy.

Serve immediately.

NUTRITION VALUE

62 Kcal, 4g fat,
1g fiber, 4g protein, 2g carbs.

PALEO PIE CRUST

This pie crust recipe has four ingredients and for all you holiday pies, no one will ever know that this is actually good for you!

MAKES 6 SERVING/ TOTAL TIME 10 MINUTE

INGREDIENTS

2 cup Almond flour

2 tbsp Coconut oil

1/4 tsp Salt

1 Egg

METHOD
STEP 1
Put all of the ingredients in a food processor and pulse until mixture forms a stiff ball.
Remove from bowl and add to a pie dish. Press into dish and use as you would any pie crust.

NUTRITION VALUE

253 Kcal, 10g fat,
7g fiber, 46g protein, 15g carbs.

PALEO SPINACH, KALE, AND ARTICHOKE DIP

Eat with sliced veggies for a wholesome snack everyone will love.

MAKES 8 SERVING/ TOTAL TIME 10 MINUTE

INGREDIENTS

1 bunch Kale (stems removed)

1 bunch Spinach (tough stems removed)

2 cloves Garlic

1 cup Artichoke hearts (drained)

2 tbsp Olive oil

2 tbsp Olive oil-based mayonnaise

1 Lime (juiced)

Sea salt an fresh ground pepper (to taste)

METHOD

STEP 1

Put the kale and spinach in a food processor and pulse until rough chopped. Add the garlic and artichoke hearts, and pulse once or twice.

STEP 2

Add the oil, mayo, and lemon juice and pulse until just combined. Season with salt and pepper to taste and serve.

NUTRITION VALUE

464 Kcal, 20g fat, 20.8g fiber, 43g protein, 8g carbs.

PALEO BLUEBERRY THYME SMOOTHIE

Full of antioxidants, this smoothie gets a unique flavor from the combination of thyme and lime juice. Perfect for a quick breakfast or afternoon snack, you'll find yourself making it again and again.

MAKES 2 SERVING/ TOTAL TIME 5 MINUTE

INGREDIENTS

1 cup Frozen blueberries

1 cup Coconut milk

1/2 tsp Thyme leaves

1 Lime (juiced)

1 Banana

METHOD

STEP 1

Put all of the ingredients in a blender and blend until smooth and creamy. Serve immediately.

NUTRITION VALUE	467 Kcal, 20g fat, 1g fiber, 48.1g protein, 3.4g carbs.

TROPICAL FRUIT SALAD

Dried papaya paired with tropical fruit is perfection when drizzled with a bit of lime juice. This salad makes the perfect snack, but can do wonders as a dessert.

MAKES 4 SERVING/ TOTAL TIME 10 MINUTE

INGREDIENTS

1 cup Strawberries (hulled and halved)

1/2 cup Papaya (dried)

1/4 cup Pumpkin seed

2 Kiwi (peeled and sliced)

1 Mango (peeled, pitted and diced)

1 Lime (juice)

METHOD
STEP 1
Put all of the ingredients in a large bowl and toss well. Serve immediately.

NUTRITION VALUE	335 Kcal, 14g fat, 8g fiber, 32g protein, 15g carbs.

PALEO SWEET AND SPICY POTATO CHIPS

Everyone loves potato chips and conforming to Paleo Diet.

MAKES 6 SERVING/ TOTAL TIME 20 MINUTE

INGREDIENTS

2 large Sweet potatoes

1/2 cup olive oil

1 tsp Chili powder

Sea salt (to taste)

METHOD

STEP 1

Peel and slice the potatoes on a mandolin slicer as thin as you can get them. Line a sheet pan with paper towels.

STEP 2

Pour about 1/2 inch of olive oil in a deep skillet. Turn the heat on medium high and allow the oil to heat up for several minutes. Add one of the chips to the oil; if it sizzles, it's ready.

Cook the potatoes in an even layer, in batches, until all are cooked. Season with chili powder and sea salt to taste and serve immediately.

NUTRITION VALUE	335 Kcal, 14g fat, 8g fiber, 32g protein, 15g carbs.

PALEO HOMEMADE APPLESAUCE

Ditch the sugary jarred variety for this homemade applesauce, and you'll never look back. You control the spices and amount of sugar, making this recipe a perfect Paleo snack.

MAKES 6 SERVING/ TOTAL TIME 45 MINUTE

INGREDIENTS

3 lbs Apples (any variety, peeled, cored, and chopped)

1/2 cup Apple cider (or water)

1 Lemon (juiced)

2-3 tbsp Honey (or maple syrup)

1/2 tsp Cinnamon

METHOD

STEP 1

Put all of the ingredients in a large pot. Bring to a boil, and reduce heat to a simmer.

Simmer for 20-30 minutes, until apples are well broken down.

STEP 2

For a chunkier applesauce, serve as is. For a smoother version, puree in a blender or food processor. Store in the fridge.

NUTRITION VALUE	625 Kcal, 20 fat, 11g fiber, 54.2g protein, 14 carbs.

BUFFALO MUSHROOM SKEWERS

Button mushrooms get coated in velvety hot sauce for a quick and easy side dish. Perfect with steaks, grilled chicken, or anything else you want to serve it with.

MAKES 6 SERVING/ TOTAL TIME 20 MINUTE

INGREDIENTS

1 pound Button mushrooms

1/2 cup Hot sauce

2 tbsp olive oil

1/2 tsp Sea salt

METHOD

STEP 1

With a paper towel, carefully clean the mushrooms, but don't get them wet. Leave whole, but remove the stems if desired.

Whisk the hot sauce, olive oil, and salt in a bowl. Add the mushrooms and toss to coat.

STEP 2

To cook the mushrooms, thread them on skewers and lay on a baking sheet (or alternatively, you can leave them off the skewers) Bake for 15 minutes in a 375 degree oven, or grill them on a grill over medium high heat. Serve warm.

NUTRITION VALUE

200 Kcal, 10g fat,
10g fiber, 20g protein, 15g carbs.

PALEO OPEN FACED PORTOBELLO SANDWICH

This is not just a normal sandwich, because it's Portobello Sandwich!

MAKES 2 SERVING/ TOTAL TIME 10 MINUTE

INGREDIENTS

2 tbsp olive oil

2 cups Baby spinach

4 slices bacon (cooked)

2 Portobello mushrooms (cleaned)

1 Avocado (pitted and sliced)

1 Lemon (juiced)

Sea salt and fresh ground pepper (to taste)

METHOD

STEP 1

Preheat broiler to high heat. Brush the mushrooms with the olive oil and season with salt and pepper. Lay on a baking sheet and broil for 4 to 5 minutes, until lightly browned. Remove from oven and let cool slightly.

STEP 2

Top each mushroom half with spinach, bacon, and avocado. Drizzle with the lemon juice before serving.

NUTRITION VALUE

353 Kcal, 15g fat, 8g fiber, 35g protein, 15g carbs.

Lightning Source UK Ltd.
Milton Keynes UK
UKHW051447090621
385129UK00002BA/167